THE OFFICIAL ENGLAND CRICKET ANNUAL 2024

WE ARE ENGLAND CRICKET

Written by Andy Greeves
Designed by Jon Dalrymple
Contributions by Cathryn Greeves and Justin Cox

A Grange Publication

Published by Grange Communications Ltd., Edinburgh. Printed in the EU.

Photographs © ECB; Getty Images; International Cricket Council (ICC)

ISBN 978-1-915879-17-2

Contents

WELCOME TO THE OFFICIAL ENGLAND CRICKET ANNUAL 2024

2024 will be another bumper year for England Men's and Women's teams as Ben Stokes' Test side welcome touring teams from the West Indies and Sri Lanka while Jos Buttler's White-Ball team head to the ICC Men's T20I World Cup in the United States and West Indies and take on Pakistan (T20I) and Australia (T20I & ODI). Heather Knight's Women's team will also face the challenge of Pakistan and New Zealand on home soil.

In this Annual, we profile both the men's and women's senior squads as well as their Head Coaches, Brendan McCullum, Matthew Mott and Jon Lewis. We also take a look back on some memorable action from 2023, including the Men's and Women's Ashes Series against old foe, Australia.

We take a look ahead to the ICC Men's T20I World Cup and we find out which iconic cricketing venues will be hosting England matches from 2025 up to and including 2031. All this, alongside other features, quizzes, games and plenty more besides to entertain England cricket fans of all ages!

COME ON ENGLAND!

www.ecb.co.uk

England Cricket

Editor Andy Greeves looks at significant moments in the history of England Men's and Women's national teams.

1739 – The first recorded incidence of an England team came from a match on 9 July 1739 when an 'All-England' Men's side took on a Kent representative XI.

1859 – England Men's first tour took place as an 'All-England XI' visited North America in September 1859.

1877 – England Men took on Australia at the Melbourne Cricket Ground on 15 March 1877 in what is recognised as the world's first Test match.

England Women's captain Mary Duggan

1882 – An Australian win over England on 29 August 1882 and a subsequent newspaper headline gave rise to a Test match series between the two nations becoming known as The Ashes.

1889 – England's 1888-89 tour of South Africa happened as the African country became the world's third recognised Test cricket nation.

1934 – The first Women's Test took place at the Brisbane Exhibition Ground on 28-31 December 1934 as England beat Australia by nine wickets.

1958 – England Women's captain and bowling legend Mary Duggan took a then-record 7-6 during the second Test against Australia in Melbourne on 21-24 February 1958.

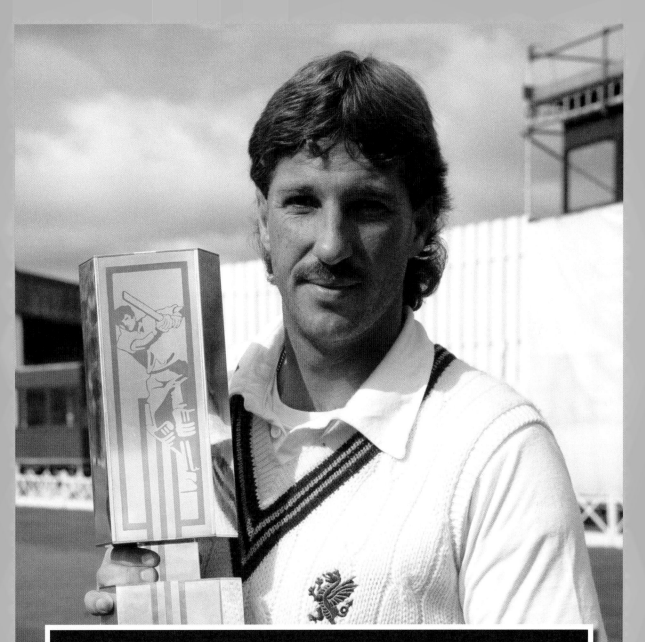

1971 – After officials abandoned the third Test between Australia and England during the 1970-71 Ashes series, a one-off, one day game which consisted of 40, eight-ball overs per side took place instead on 5 January 1971. One Day International (ODI) cricket was born!

1973 – England Women played their first Women's One Day International (WODI) against an International XI at County Cricket Ground in Hove on 23 June 1973. The team hosted and won the inaugural ICC Women's World Cup that same year.

1975 – England hosted the first ICC World Cup between 7-21 June 1975, won by the West Indies.

1977 – England legend Sir Ian Botham made the first of his 102 Test appearances against Australia on 28 July 1977.

Graham Gooch

1980 – Botham became just the second player in Test history to complete a 'match double' (scoring over 100 runs and taking 10 wickets in the same match) against India on 15-19 February 1980. In the same match, Graham Gooch achieved the most runs of any player in an international Test match with a score of 456 (333 and 123).

1981 – Botham helped England come from behind as his 149* against Australia inspired victory in the third Test of the 1981 Ashes series known as 'Botham's Ashes'.

1993 – England hosted and triumphed at the 1993 ICC Women's Cricket World Cup, which was played between 20 July and 1 August 1993.

1997 - The England and Wales Cricket Board (ECB), the national governing body for cricket in England and Wales, was founded on 1 January 1997.

2003 - A shortened cricket format called Twenty20 (T20) was introduced by the ECB in 2003, with matches featuring a single innings for each team, restricted to a maximum of 20 overs.

2005 – England Men ended their 18-year wait for an Ashes Series victory, with a 2-1 triumph on home soil in 2005. A three-wicket win at Trent Bridge in the fourth Test and a draw in the final match at the Oval secured the urn for Michael Vaughan's side.

2007 – England Men competed in the inaugural ICC T20I World Cup, staged in South Africa from 11-24 September 2007.

2009 – England Women beat 2009 ICC Women's Cricket World Cup hosts Australia in the final of the tournament to win the competition for a third time.

2010 - England Men's first success in the ICC T20I World Cup came when Paul Collingwood skippered the side to victory and scored the winning run in the final to seal a seven-wicket victory over Australia in the West Indies on 16 May 2010.

2011 - Alastair Cook hit 294 runs off 545 balls as England made 710-7 in the third Test against India on 10-14 August 2011.

2017 – England's success at the ICC Women's Cricket World Cup continued in 2017 with a fourth tournament triumph.

2019 – England hosted the 2019 ICC Cricket World Cup and won the competition for the first time with victory over New Zealand in the final at Lord's on 14 July 2019.

2022 – England Men won the ICC T20I World Cup for a second time in their history with a five-wicket success against Pakistan in the final of the competition staged in Australia between 16 October and 13 November 2022. More details can be found on pages 48-51.

2023 – A thrilling joint Men's & Women's Ashes Series ended with draws for both sides; the Men's team drawing 2-2 in the Test series whilst the Women's team drew 8-8 in the points-based Women's Ashes system. More details can be found on pages 54-59.

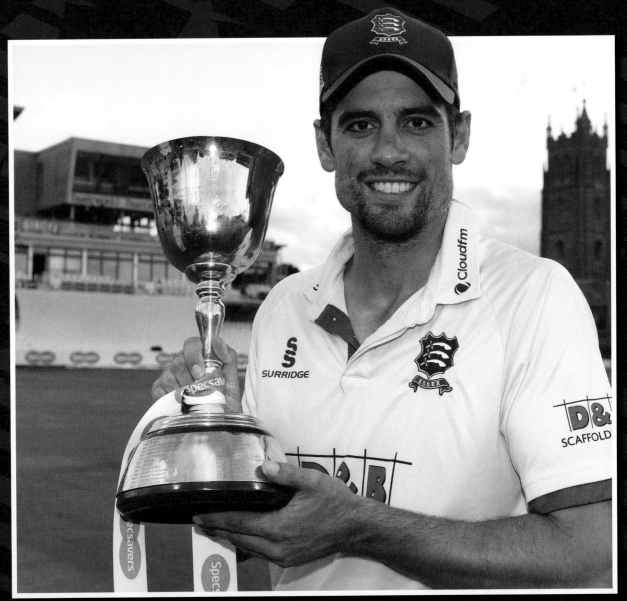

Alastair Cook

SPOT THE DIFFERENCE

Can you find the eight differences in the two pictures below?

Find the solution on page 61

SPOT THE BALL

Can you spot which is the correct ball in the picture below?

WORD GRID

Arrange the surnames of the following England Men's and Women's players into the grid to reveal the surname of an England Women's player.

AHMED
DUCKETT
ROOT
BAIRSTOW
WINFIELD-HILL
WONG

Find the solution on page 61

ENGLAND MEN'S TEAM...

Information correct as of 31 July 2023 (Up to and including the result of the fifth Test v Australia in July 2023)

PERSONNEL

COACH – Brendon McCullum

ONE DAY & T20I COACH – Matthew Mott

TEST CAPTAIN – Ben Stokes

ONE DAY CAPTAIN – Jos Buttler

T20I CAPTAIN - Jos Buttler

TESTS

TEST STATUS ACQUIRED - 1877

FIRST INTERNATIONAL v Australia at the Melbourne Cricket Ground, Melbourne, 15-19 March 1877

TEST RECORD – Played 1,066, Won 391, Drawn 355, Lost 320

WORLD TEST CHAMPIONSHIP BEST RESULT – Fourth in 2019-2021 and 2021-2023 (World Test Championship Debut)

ONE DAY INTERNATIONALS

FIRST ODI v Australia at the Melbourne Cricket Ground, Melbourne, 5 January 1971

ODI RECORD – Played 779, Won 392, Lost 348 (9 ties and 30 no result)

CRICKET WORLD CUP BEST RESULT – Winners 2019

TWENTY20 INTERNATIONALS

FIRST T20I v Australia at the Ageas Bowl, Southampton, 13 June 2005

T20I RECORD – Played 173, Won 90, Lost 75 (2 ties and 6 no result)

T20I WORLD CUP BEST RESULT – Winners 2010 and 2022

PLAYER RECORDS

MOST CAREER TEST APPEARANCES – James Anderson – 183 matches (2003-to date)

MOST CAREER TEST RUNS – Alastair Cook – 12,472 runs in 161 matches (2006-2018)

MOST CAREER TEST WICKETS – James Anderson - 690 wickets in 183 matches (2003-to date)

HEAD COACH PROFILES

BRENDON McCULLUM

Full Name: Brendon Barrie McCullum
Date of Birth: 27 September 1981
Place of Birth: Dunedin, Otago, New Zealand
England Men's Head Coach: Since 12 May 2022

One of the most renowned players in New Zealand's history, Brendon McCullum played over 100 Test matches between 2004 and 2016.

During his career, the right-handed opening batter broke the world record for the fastest Test century on 20 February 2016 as he took just 54 balls to reach 100 on day one of the second Test against Australia in Christchurch. McCullum surpassed West Indies legend Vivian Richards in the process – who had previously hit 145 off 79 balls against England in 1986. He achieved his 12th Test ton - hitting 16 fours and four sixes - in his last match before retirement from international cricket.

Amongst McCullum's 12 tons was a score of 302 against India on 18 February 2014, which saw him become the first New Zealander to score a triple-hundred. That same year, he became the first New Zealander to score 1,000 test runs in a calendar year with a total of 1,164.

McCullum excelled at the white-ball game too. He led the Kiwi's to the finals of the 2015 Cricket World Cup, where they lost to Australia by 7 wickets. He is the former leading run scorer in Twenty20 International (T20I) cricket (having 2,410 runs between 2005 and 2015) and one of only two New Zealanders – the other being Martin Guptill - to have scored two T20I centuries and 2,000 runs in T20I.

McCullum's other achievements in T20I included him becoming the first batsman to score two tons, and being the previous record holder for the highest individual score in a T20I match with 123 against Bangladesh in 2012. He hit the then-third highest individual score in all Twenty20 cricket in 2008 with 158 not out for the Kolkata Knight Riders against the Royal Challengers Bangalore

McCullum retired from all forms of cricket in 2019 and was appointed as Head Coach of both Trinbago Knight Riders and Kolkata Knight Riders in August that year. He led Trinbago Knight Riders to their fourth Caribbean Premier League (CPL)

McCullum was appointed as England Head Coach on 12 May 2022. Just a month on, his new team went on to secure a three-Test match series clean sweep against New Zealand. That same summer, England chased down a national record 378 for the loss of only three wickets to beat India in the fifth Test at Edgbaston in 2022.

Progress continued later in the year as England enjoyed a 2-1 series win against South African on home soil while they also achieved a first-ever whitewash of Pakistan in a home series in the winter of 2022.

MATTHEW MOTT

Full Name: Matthew Peter Mott
Date of Birth: 3 October 1973
Place of Birth: Charleville, Queensland, Australia
England Men's White-Ball Head Coach:
Since 18 May 2022

Just six months on from his appointment as England Men's White-Ball Head Coach, Australian Matthew Mott coached the England T20I side to victory at the 2022 ICC T20I World Cup, which was staged in his homeland between 16 October and 13 November 2022 (more details on this triumph can be found on pages 48-51 of this Annual).

Mott joined England's coaching set-up days after Brendon McCullum became Test Head Coach in May 2022. He penned a contract to take charge of both the Men's T20I and ODI teams through until 2026.

Mott's coaching experience began in 2007 in his native Australia with New South Wales, who he led to Champions League T20I glory two years later. He departed New South Wales for Glamorgan in 2011, who reached the final of the Yorkshire Bank 40 in 2013. He worked as a consultant for Ireland during the 2015 ICC Men's World Cup before becoming Australia Women Head Coach that same year.

During the former Queensland and Victoria left-handed batter's seven-year tenure, Australia Women won consecutive ICC T20I World Cups, the 2022 ICC Women's 50-Over World Cup and were undefeated in four Ashes series. Mott has also helped Australia win 26 consecutive ODIs - a

ENGLAND MEN'S TEAM PROFILES

BEN STOKES

Role: Left-handed batter, right-arm fast medium bowler, Test captain

DOB: 4 June 1991

POB: Christchurch, New Zealand

Intl. debut: 25 August 2011 v Ireland (ODI; Dublin)

In the first Test against New Zealand in February 2023, Ben surpassed England Head Coach Brendon McCullum's record of 107 sixes to become the highest six hitter in Test cricket history. England's captain also enjoyed a solid performance in that summer's Ashes as he hit a series total of 405 runs during a year in which he was also named the Wisden Leading Cricketer in the World for a third time. Having established himself in English cricketing folklore for his Man of the Match performance against his native New Zealand in the 2019 ICC ODI Cricket World Cup Final, he was also a key member of the England squad that won the 2022 ICC T20I World Cup. In August 2023, he came out of ODI retirement ahead of the 2023 ICC ODI Cricket World Cup.

OLLIE POPE

Role: Right-handed batter, Test vice-captain

DOB: 2 January 1998

POB: Chelsea, London

Intl. debut: 9 August 2018 v India (Test; Lord's)

Appointed England's vice-captain in 2023, Ollie was in great form going into the year's Ashes Series, having hit 205 runs off 208 balls at Lord's in the 10-wicket Test victory over Ireland in June – and being named Man of the Match in the process. But an injury sustained in the second Test against Australia at Lord's saw his Ashes end early. Such set-backs are nothing new to Ollie but he has shown time and time again his ability to bounce back. When England toured South Africa in 2019-20 for example, he missed the first Test through injury only to return to hit 61* in the second Test before grabbing his first Test century - 135* at Port Elizabeth - in the third.

REHAN AHMED

Role: Right-handed batter, right-arm leg-spin bowler
DOB: 13 August 2004
POB: Nottingham, Nottinghamshire
Intl. debut: 17 December 2022 v Pakistan (Test; Karachi)

In December 2022, Rehan became the youngest man ever to play Test cricket for England as he debuted against Pakistan in Karachi at the age of 18 years and 126 days. He marked the occasion with a five-wicket haul in the host's second innings to help seal a 74-run victory. In the process, he became the youngest debutant to achieve a five-wicket haul in men's Tests. The 2022 BBC Young Sports Personality of the Year nominee continued to set records in 2023 as he became England's youngest ODI and T20I debutant in matches against Bangladesh aged 18 years and 205/211 days respectively.

JAMES ANDERSON

Role: Right-arm fast medium bowler
DOB: 30 July 1982
POB: Burnley, Lancashire
Intl. debut: 15 December 2002 v Australia (ODI; Melbourne)

As he prepares to celebrate his 42nd birthday in July 2024, James continues to be a vital member of England's Test squad. His country's all-time leading Test wicket-taker, with 690 scalps to his name by the end of the 2023 Ashes series and a record 269 wickets in ODIs, the Lancastrian is one of the finest bowlers the sport has ever seen. He had 183 caps at the time of writing with only Sachin Tendulkar having played more Test matches than James. From a five-wicket haul against Zimbabwe on his Test debut back in May 2003 to a double five-wicket haul against Pakistan in 2010 for just 71 runs, James' international career has produced a catalogue of highlights. Unsurprisingly, on the occasion of England's 1,000th Test back in 2018, he was included in the ECB's greatest all-time Test XI.

JONNY BAIRSTOW

Role: Right-handed batter; wicketkeeper
DOB: 26 September 1989
POB: Bradford, West Yorkshire
Intl. debut: 16 September 2011 v India (ODI; Cardiff)

Jonny's sporting talent was obvious from an early age as he attended Leeds United FC's youth academy and was named Young Wisden Schools Cricketer of the Year after scoring 654 runs for St Peter's School in York in 2007. The wicket-keeper-batter debuted in international white-ball cricket in 2011 and made his first Test appearance against the West Indies in May 2012. A key member of the team ever since, Jonny was just five matches short of a century of Test appearances at the time of writing. A member of England's 2019 ICC ODI World Cup, the Yorkshireman - along with Ben Stokes - holds the world record for the highest sixth-wicket stand in Tests: 399 against South Africa during England's 2015-16 tour.

HARRY BROOK

Role: Right-handed batter; right-arm medium bowler
DOB: 22 February 1999
POB: Keighley, West Yorkshire
Intl. debut: 26 January 2022 v West Indies (T20I; Barbados)

Harry's introduction to Test cricket has been spectacular to say the least, with the West Yorkshire-born player amassing 809 runs in his first six appearances. During that time, he hit 153, 108 and 111 respectively during England's tour of Pakistan in 2022-23 as he was unsurprisingly named Player of the Series. His heroics continued during the second and final Test match against New Zealand at Basin Reserve in February 2023 as he managed a score of 186. He also scored 75 to help England win the third Test match against Australia during the 2023 Ashes Series. In that innings, he became the fastest batter (by balls faced) to 1,000 runs in Test cricket history.

JOS BUTTLER

Role: Right-handed batter; wicketkeeper, white-ball captain
DOB: 8 September 1990
POB: Taunton, Somerset
Intl. debut: 31 August 2011 v India (T20I; Manchester)

Following Eoin Morgan's retirement in 2022, Jos became England's new white-ball captain after serving for seven years as vice-skipper. His appointment was an obvious choice having been a top-level performer for England in all formats of the game - especially T20I and ODI - since 2011. England's second-most capped T20I player, the wicket-keeper-batter is England's highest run-scorer in T20Is and, at the time of writing, one of only four Englishmen to score a T20I century and, as wicket keeper, holds the country's T20I and ODI records for most dismissals. Vice-captain of England's 2019 ICC World Cup-winning team and skipper of the victorious 2022 ICC T20I World Cup side, Jos - along with Adil Rashid - holds the world record for the highest seventh-wicket stand in ODIs: 177 achieved against New Zealand in 2015.

ZAK CRAWLEY

Role: Right-handed batter
DOB: 3 February 1998
POB: Bromley, London
Intl. debut: 29 November 2019 v New Zealand (Test; Hamilton)

Zak was described as "a magnificent player" by cricketing royalty Sir Viv Richards during England's tour of the West Indies in 2022 where he managed his second Test century with a score of 121 in the first Test in Antigua. His first Test century came in August 2020 when he scored 267 off just 393 balls against Pakistan and 320 runs in total during the three-match series. It was a shame that his incredible innings against Pakistan came behind closed doors at the Rose Bowl in Southampton as part of measures introduced in the midst of the COVID-19 pandemic.

SAM CURRAN

Role: Left-arm fast bowler; left-handed batter
DOB: 3 June 1998
POB: Northampton, Northamptonshire
Intl. debut: 1 June 2018 v Pakistan (Test; Leeds)

A fine all-rounder, Sam was named Player of the Tournament as England won the 2022 ICC T20I World Cup as he took 13 wickets in six matches. Sam is from a cricketing family, with his dad Kevin M Curran and grandfather Kevin P Curran having played for Zimbabwe and the former Rhodesia respectively while he is the younger brother of Surrey and England teammate Tom Curran. Sam holds the English record for the best T20I bowling figures: 5–10 against Afghanistan in 2022. He was also the subject of the highest bid in the history of the Indian Premier League in December 2022 as he joined the Punjab Kings for a reported £1.85m fee.

BEN DUCKETT

Role: Left-handed batter; wicketkeeper
DOB: 17 October 1994
POB: Farnborough, London
Intl. debut: 7 October 2016 v Bangladesh (ODI; Mirpur)

Debuting alongside Jake Ball in England's 21-run ODI victory over Bangladesh in 2016, Ben had featured in 15 Test matches and six ODIs by early August 2023. Viewed as a player well-suited to the 'Bazball' style of play introduced by England captain Ben Stokes and Head Coach Brendon McCullum, Ben was called up for the tour of Pakistan in late 2022. His selection paid off handsomely as, along with Zak Crawley, he scored the fastest ever England century opening stand off 83 balls. The pair also went on to achieve the fastest double-century partnership in Test cricket history off 233 balls.

MOEEN ALI

Role: Left-handed batter, right-arm offspin bowler
DOB: 18 June 1987
POB: Birmingham
Intl. debut: 28 February 2014 v West Indies (ODI; North Sound)

Moeen briefly came out of Test retirement for The Ashes in the summer of 2023 after an injury to Jack Leach. After taking three wickets on the final day of the series, as England beat Australia by 49 runs at The Kia Oval, the all-rounder confirmed he would once again be retiring from Test cricket after 3,094 runs and 204 wickets in 68 matches. He will continue to be an important member of Jos Buttler's white-ball team, with outings against Bangladesh (ODI) in March 2023 and New Zealand (T20I) in August 2023 making his 129th ODI and 74th T20I appearances respectively. He was a member of England's winning squads at the 2019 ICC Cricket World Cup and the 2022 ICC Men's T20I World Cup.

JACK LEACH

Role: Left-arm spin bowler
DOB: 22 June 1991
POB: Taunton, Somerset
Intl. debut: 30 March 2018 v New Zealand (Test; Christchurch)

Jack ended 2022 as the third-highest wicket taker in the world, behind only Kagiso Rabada and Nathan Lyon. He took his first ten-wicket haul against New Zealand in June 2022 and then, in the 2022–23 winter, took 25 wickets across five tests against Pakistan and New Zealand, including a five-wicket haul in Wellington. Expected to have an influential Ashes in 2023, Jack experienced back pain during the first Test match of that summer and was sadly ruled out of the series with a stress fracture. The player achieved cult-like status back in 2019 when he scored a run described by *The Guardian* as "arguably the greatest one not out in the history of the game" in his last-wicket partnership with Ben Stokes as England beat Australia by one wicket in the third Ashes Test at Headingley.

MATTHEW POTTS

Role: Right-arm fast medium bowler
DOB: 29 October 1998
POB: Sunderland, Tyne and Wear
Intl. debut: 2 June 2022 v New Zealand (Test; Lord's)

Matty made an impressive international debut in May 2022 as he took 4-13 in the first innings against New Zealand in the first Test at Lord's. He followed that up with 3-55 in the second innings. The Sunderland-born bowler was subsequently named in England's squad for their ODI home series against South Africa and made his debut in that form of international cricket at Chester-le-Street a month after making his Test bow. Potts' selection for England came on from his excellent displays of pace-bowling for Durham where he plays alongside Test captain Ben Stokes.

ADIL RASHID

Role: Right-arm leg-spin bowler
DOB: 17 February 1988
POB: Bradford, West Yorkshire
Intl. debut: 5 June 2009 v Netherlands (T20I; Lord's)

Awarded an MBE in King Charles III's birthday honour's list in 2023, Adil is England's highest wicket-taker among spin bowlers in both ODIs and T20Is and the second-highest wicket-taker in T20Is after Chris Jordan. Along with Jos Buttler, he also holds the record for the highest seventh-wicket stand in ODIs: 177 against New Zealand in 2015. He was an integral part of Eoin Morgan's side that won the 2019 ICC Cricket World Cup and was named in England's squad for the 2021 ICC Men's T20I World Cup. Rashid is an Ambassador for the Overseas Plastic Surgery Appeal charity who provide free facial surgery for poor children and young adults in Pakistan where the bowler's family hail from.

OLLIE ROBINSON

Role: Right-arm medium-fast bowler
DOB: 1 December 1993
POB: Sidcup, London
Intl. debut: 2 June 2021 v New Zealand (Test; Lord's)

Ollie made his international debut alongside James Bracey in the first Test of New Zealand's tour of England in the summer of 2021. Later that year he took his first five-wicket Test haul against India at Trent Bridge. He was England's leading wicket taker in the summer of 2022 taking 28 wickets for an average of 19.60. His performances for his country and county side Sussex had seen him named as one of Wisden's five Cricketers of the Year earlier in the year. He brought his Test cap tally to 19 during the 2023 Ashes Series.

JOE ROOT

Role: Right-handed batter; right-arm spin bowler
DOB: 30 December 1990
POB: Sheffield, South Yorkshire
Intl. debut: 13 December 2012 v India (Test; Nagpur)

During his tenure as England's Test team captain between February 2017 and April 2022, Joe skippered in more Test matches (64) than any other player and also oversaw most Test victories, with 27. He was the leading run-scorer as England won the 2019 ICC ODI World Cup and, in June 2022, became just the second England batter after Sir Alastair Cook to score 10,000 Test runs. He was tenth on the list of top Test run scorers at the time of writing with the tallies of legends of the game such as Mahela Jayawardene, Shivnarine Chanderpaul and Brian Lara in his sights. There has been no shortage of personal accolades for Joe, who was named both the ICC Men's Test Cricketer of the Year and the Wisden Leading Cricketer in the World in 2021. He was also included in the ECB's greatest all-time Test XI back in 2018.

JOSH TONGUE

Role: Right-arm fast bowler; right-handed batter
DOB: 15 November 1997
POB: Redditch, Worcestershire
Intl. debut: 1 June 2023 v Ireland (Test; Lord's)

A star performer for Worcestershire over the years, Josh announced himself at international level in 2023 with his debut against Ireland followed by an England call-up for the 2023 Ashes Series. Known affectionately by his teammates as 'Jeevy Boy', Josh took his maiden Test wicket against Ireland as he went on to finish the innings with figures of 5-66 in that match. The fast-bowler featured in the second Test against Australia on 28 June-2 July 2023 and duly took 3-98 in the first innings at Lord's.

CHRIS WOAKES

Role: Right-arm fast bowler; right-handed batter
DOB: 2 March 1989
POB: Birmingham
Intl. debut: 12 January 2011 v Australia (T20I; Adelaide)

A key member of England's team that won the 2019 ICC Cricket World Cup, the reliable all-rounder played in all 11 matches at the tournament, taking 16 wickets and scoring 149 runs. He is one of just six players to have been part of both that triumph and England's success at the 2022 ICC T20I World Cup. A classy lower-order batter, often scoring vital runs, Chris has six Test 50s to his name at the time of writing while he scored 137* in an innings victory over India at Lord's in 2018. After taking 19 wickets in the six innings he played, Chris was named England's Player of the Series in the 2023 Ashes.

MARK WOOD

Role: Right-arm fast bowler
DOB: 11 January 1990
POB: Ashington, Northumberland
Intl. debut: 8 May 2015 v Ireland (ODI; Dublin)

A focal point of England's attack in both red and white ball cricket, the Northumberland-born player was crucial to tournament successes at the 2019 ICC ODI World Cup and 2022 ICC T20I World Cup. His 18 wickets at the 2019 ICC ODI World Cup came at a strike-rate of 29.8, giving England the ability to break partnerships in the middle overs. He also played in every Super 12 game in Australia before succumbing to injury and missing out on the semi-final and final. Recalled to the England squad for the third Test of the 2023 Ashes Series, Mark was named Man of the Match as he took a collective 7-100 and scored 40 runs from 16 balls.

ENGLAND WOMEN'S TEAM..

Information correct as of 18 July 2023 (including the final WODI v Australia)

PERSONNEL

COACH – Jon Lewis

CAPTAIN – Heather Knight

WOMEN'S TESTS

FIRST WTEST v Australia at the Brisbane Exhibition Ground, Brisbane, 28–31 December 1934

TEST RECORD – Played 99, Won 20, Drawn 64, Lost 15

WOMEN'S ONE DAY INTERNATIONALS

FIRST WODI v International XI at County Cricket Ground, Hove, 23 June 1973

WODI RECORD – Played 383, Won 225, Lost 145 (2 ties and 11 no result)

WOMEN'S CRICKET WORLD CUP BEST RESULT – Winners 1973, 1993, 2009 and 2017

WOMEN'S TWENTY20 INTERNATIONALS

FIRST WT20I v New Zealand at County Cricket Ground, Hove, 5 August 2004

WT20I RECORD – Played 181, Won 130, Lost 46 (3 ties and 2 no result)

WOMEN'S T20I WORLD CUP BEST RESULT – Winners 2009

PLAYER RECORDS

MOST CAREER WOMEN'S TEST APPEARANCES – Jan Brittin – 27 matches (1979-1998)

MOST CAREER WOMEN'S TEST RUNS – Jan Brittin – 1,935 runs in 27 matches (1979-1998)

MOST CAREER WOMEN'S TEST WICKETS – Mary Duggan - 77 wickets in 17 matches (1949-1963)

HEAD COACH PROFILE
JON LEWIS

Full Name:
Jonathan Lewis

Date of Birth:
26 August 1975

Place of Birth:
Aylesbury, Buckinghamshire

England Women's Head Coach:
Since 18 November 2022

After a period as the ECB's Elite Pace Bowling Coach, working alongside the England Men's Test and white-ball teams, Jon Lewis became Head Coach of England Women in November 2022 as he succeeded Australian Lisa Keightley. Lewis had previously served as Head Coach of the Young Lions, having joined the ECB from the coaching staff at Sussex CCC back in 2016.

Lewis' first assignment as England Women Head Coach saw him travel to the Caribbean with his new team where they played three Women's One Day Internationals (WODIs) and five Women's Twenty20 Internationals (WT20Is) against the West Indies. England enjoyed a series sweep winning 3-0 in the WODI series and 6-0 in the WT20I series.

England made a good start to 2023 by reaching the semi-finals of the ICC Women's T20I World Cup (see pages 32-35 for more information). While Australia were triumphant in the one and only Test match in the 2023 Women's Ashes series, England won the WODI and WT20I series 2-1 (more information on pages 54-58). The Ashes series ended as a draw therefore, with both teams earning eight points.

Before getting into coaching, Lewis took over 1,200 professional wickets in a 19-year professional career at Gloucestershire, Surrey and Sussex, and played 15 times for his country. His solitary Test appearance came against Sri Lanka in 2006; he was also included in England's 15-man squad for the ICC Cricket World Cup a year later.

Lewis played for Gloucestershire for 16 years between 1995 and 2011, before spending two seasons with Surrey and his final campaign as a professional with Sussex in 2014. He was appointed as Assistant Head Coach at Sussex a year later before starting his aforementioned role with the Young Lions in 2016 and was a Bowling Coach with Sri Lanka between 2019 and 2021. His stint as the ECB's Elite Pace Bowling Coach, meanwhile, saw him work with the likes of Jofra Archer, Mark Wood and Ben Stokes.

Lewis' most recent appointment came in February 2023 as he became Head Coach of UP Warriorz in the inaugural Indian Women's Premier League – a role he will combine with his position with England Women.

ENGLAND WOMEN'S TEAM PROFILES

HEATHER KNIGHT

Role: Right-handed batter

DOB: 26 December 1990

POB: Plymouth, Devon

Intl. debut: 1 March 2010 v India (ODI; Mumbai)

England Women captain since 2016, Heather led her team to glory at the 2017 ICC Women's Cricket World Cup – one of ten major tournaments she has appeared in as of July 2023. During that time, her team have been runners-up in the 2022 ICC Women's Cricket World Cup and finalists in the ICC Women's T20I World Cup on three occasions. A middle-order batter, Heather leads from the front as a mountainous run-scorer. She is one of only two female players (the other being Tammy Beaumont) to have scored centuries in all three formats of the game. Heather was awarded with an OBE (Order of the British Empire) in the Queen's 2018 New Year's Honours list.

NAT SCIVER-BRUNT

Role: Right-arm medium bowler, right-handed batter

DOB: 20 August 1992

POB: Tokyo, Japan

Intl. debut: 1 July 2013 v Pakistan (WODI; Louth)

A world-class all-rounder, Nat demonstrated her brilliance with the bat during the 2023 Ashes as she helped England to a 2-1 victory in the three-match WODI series with 271 including 129 off 149 balls in the third and final WODI in Taunton on 18 July. The same series saw the skiddy medium pacer take two wickets for 38 runs in the first WODI. Nat leads the ICC ODI all-round rankings at the time of writing, with a career-best 402 rating coming against Australia on 16 July 2023. The first English cricketer to take a T20I hat-trick, her brilliant 148* in the 2022 ICC Women's World Cup Final was sadly in vain as England went down to a 71-run defeat to Australia in Christchurch.

MAIA BOUCHIER

Role: **Right-handed batter**

DOB: **5 December 1998**

POB: **Kensington, London**

Intl. debut: **4 September 2021 v New Zealand (WT20I; Hove)**

Maia's impressive showing in the WT20I series against the West Indies in December 2022 – a series in which she played in every match and scored 31 runs in three innings – ensured the hard-hitting middle-order batter a place in England Women's WT20I squads for the 2023 ICC Women's T20I World Cup and the 2023 Women's Ashes. Maia played every game for the Melbourne Stars in the 2021 Big Bash, earning a stint for Western Australia. She also shone at the 2022 Commonwealth Games in Birmingham, where she featured in every match for England.

SOPHIA DUNKLEY

Role: **Right-handed batter; right-arm spin bowler**

DOB: **16 July 1998**

POB: **Lambeth, London**

Intl. debut: **12 November 2018 v Bangladesh (WT20I; Gros Islet)**

Sophia's pioneering involvement in cricket goes back to her school days when she became the first girl to play in the boys' first XI at Mill Hill School in London. She made her senior debut for Middlesex in 2012 at the age of just 14 and played for England for the first time six years later. Awarded her first central contract in 2021, Sophia became the first black woman to play Test cricket for England - against India in June that same year. In the years since, Sophia has cemented herself as one of England's core playing group and has backed up selection with gutsy, enterprising runs in the middle-order.

DANIELLE WYATT

Role: **Right-handed batter**

DOB: **22 April 1991**

POB: **Stoke-on-Trent, Staffordshire**

Intl. debut: **1 March 2010 v India (WODI; Mumbai)**

Having represented England in the white-ball game for over a decade, 2023 marked a big year for Danni as she made her Test debut against Australia on 22 June. The opening batter was a member of England's ICC World Cup-winning squad that triumphed on home soil in 2017 – one of nine major international tournaments she has appeared in to date, as well as the 2022 Commonwealth Games. At the time of writing, Danni has two centuries to her name in both WODI and WT20I matches. 129 off 125 balls against South Africa in the 2022 World Cup semi-finals helped England into the final.

TAMMY BEAUMONT

Role: Right-handed batter; wicketkeeper

DOB: 11 March 1991

POB: Dover, Kent

Intl. debut: 4 November 2009 v West Indies (WODI; Basseterre)

In June 2023, Tammy made history when she became the first English female cricketer to hit a double century as she finished with 208 against Australia. She eclipsed Betty Snowball's previous highest score record for England Women, achieved way back in 1935. In the process, she also became just the second England Women player to achieve a century in all three international formats of the game. Named Player of the Series as England triumphed at the 2017 ICC Women's World Cup, Tammy hit the most runs at that tournament with her 410 including a 49 off 88 balls in a 3-run victory over Australia on 9 July 2017.

AMY JONES

Role: Wicketkeeper, right-handed batter

DOB: 13 June 1993

POB: Solihull, West Midlands

Intl. debut: 1 February 2013 v Sri Lanka (WODI; Mumbai)

A regular behind the stumps for England from around 2018 onwards, Amy has also impressed with the bat over the years, with memorable displays including 94 runs from 119 balls in the third WODI against India in Nagpur on 12 April 2018. She opened the batting in the 2020 ICC Women's T20I World Cup but settled into the middle-order during the 2022 ICC Women's World Cup campaign. The former Loughborough student was appointed as England's captain for the WT20I and WODI series against India in September 2022 in the absence of Nat Sciver-Brunt.

LAUREN WINFIELD-HILL

Role: Right-handed batter

DOB: 16 August 1990

POB: York, North Yorkshire

Intl. debut: 1 July 2013 v Pakistan (WODI; Louth)

Another member of England's World Cup-winning class of 2017, Lauren has been involved in the international game for over a decade having made her debut in the same WODI as Natalie Sciver-Brunt back in 2013. In her 16th year with Yorkshire at the time of writing, Lauren was also representing Northern Diamonds in the Women's Cricket Super League, Oval Invincibles in The Hundred and Melbourne Stars in the Big Bash. She has previously turned out for Northern Superchargers, Brisbane Heat, Hobart Hurricanes and Adelaide Strikers.

ALICE CAPSEY

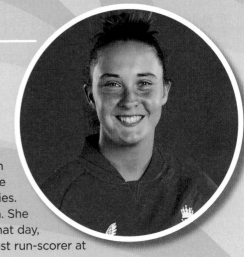

Role: Right-handed batter, right-arm off break bowler
DOB: 11 August 2004
POB: Redhill, Surrey
Intl. debut: 23 July 2022 v South Africa (WT20I; Worcester)

A real rising star, Alice was voted the inaugural PCA Women's Young Player of the Year in 2021. That same year she was named in England's A squad for the tour to Australia where she played in five matches and top-scored in the first WT20I with 44 from 31 deliveries. Alice made her WT20I debut on 23 July 2022 against South Africa. She didn't bat in the match but took her maiden international wicket that day, dismissing Lara Goodall. Alice went on to become England's highest run-scorer at the 2022 Commonwealth Games with 135 runs in five matches.

ALICE DAVIDSON-RICHARDS

Role: Right-handed batter, right-arm medium bowler
DOB: 29 May 1994
POB: Tunbridge Wells, Kent
Intl. debut: 23 March 2018 v Australia (WT20I; Mumbai)

Educated at Epsom College in Surrey, where she played cricket alongside her future England teammate Nat Sciver-Brunt, Alice has been a regular feature of Kent's teams in both formats. She won the Women's County Championship in 2011, 2012, 2014, 2016 and 2019 with her home county as well as the Women's Twenty20 Cup in 2011, 2013 and 2016. At international level, Alice made her England debut during the 2017-18 Tri-Nation Series while her Test bow came against South Africa on 27 June 2022.

EMMA LAMB

Role: Right-handed batter, right-arm off break bowler

DOB: 16 December 1997

POB: Preston, Lancashire

Intl debut: 1 September 2021 v New Zealand (WT20I; Chelmsford)

Sister of Danny Lamb, who was also playing first class cricket for Lancashire at the time of writing, Emma followed up on her 2021 WT20I debut with Test and WODI bows in 2022. Her first WODI came against South Africa in July 2022 as she hit 102 off 97 deliveries in a five-wicket victory for England. Awarded a central contract in November 2022, Emma was playing her club cricket with Lancashire, North West Thunder and Manchester Originals at the time of writing.

LAUREN BELL

Role: Right-arm fast bowler

DOB: 2 January 2001

POB: Swindon, Wiltshire

Intl debut: 27 June 2022 v South Africa (Test; Taunton)

Lauren is a multi-talented sportswoman, who made her Women's County Championship debut for Berkshire at the age of just 14 while she was a member of Reading FC's academy until the age of 16. Lauren built on impressive showings for England A to gain her full international debut against South Africa in a Test match in June 2022. In 2023, the player nicknamed 'The Shard' (due to standing 6ft tall!) played in the Test match, three WT20I and three WODI fixtures during Australia's tour of England.

KATE CROSS

Role: Right-arm medium fast bowler

DOB: 3 October 1991

POB: Manchester

Intl debut: 24 October 2013 v West Indies (WT20I; Bridgetown)

The daughter of former professional footballer and FA Cup winner David Cross, Kate was the first woman to be accepted into Lancashire CCC's academy back in 2006. A year later she won the Eversheds Most Promising Young Cricketer Award and gained her first England Under-21 cap. She made quite an introduction at senior international level taking 4-51 in the second game of the series against the West Indies in Bridgetown in October 2013 just a few months on from her debut. Kate has featured in many England squads since, gaining selection for the ICC Women's T20I World Cup in 2020 and 2023 and the ICC Women's World Cup in 2022.

FREYA DAVIES

Role: Right-arm fast medium bowler

DOB: 27 October 1995

POB: Chichester, West Sussex

Intl debut: 24 March 2019 v Sri Lanka (WT20I; Colombo)

Still awaiting her Test debut at the time of writing, Freya made her international breakthrough in both white-ball formats in 2019. She was England's joint-leading wicket-taker in the WT20I series when England toured New Zealand in 2021 and she took her best WT20I bowling figures of 4-23 in the second match of the series in Wellington. Freya was a member of England's squad that featured as runners-up in the 2022 ICC Women's Cricket World Cup and was in the travelling parties for the 2020 and 2023 ICC Women's T20I World Cup.

LAUREN FILER

Role: Right-arm fast bowler, right-handed batter

DOB: 22 December 2000

POB: Bristol

Intl debut: 22 June 2023 v Australia (Test; Nottingham)

Bristol-born Lauren made her England debut in the one and only Test of the 2023 Women Ashes series against Australia at Trent Bridge. She took four wickets in the match, two in each innings. She was subsequently named in the WODI squad for the same series, but did not feature in any of those matches. Lauren, who represents Somerset and Western Storm at the time of writing, signed her maiden professional contract with Storm at the end of the 2022 season along with Sophia Smale and Chloe Skelton.

DANIELLE GIBSON

Role: Right-arm medium bowler, right-handed batter

DOB: 30 April 2001

POB: Cheltenham, Gloucestershire

Intl debut: 1 July 2023 v Australia (WT20I; Birmingham)

Danielle was named in an England squad for the first time in January 2023 as she was a travelling reserve for the 2023 ICC Women's T20I World Cup in South Africa. Later that year, the bowler was included in the squad once again for the Ashes Series against Australia. She featured in three matches during the WT20I series, which saw her take two wickets. She achieved 4* in the third WT20I as England wrapped up a five-wicket victory (DLS method).

ISSY WONG

Role: Right-arm fast bowler

DOB: 15 May 2002

POB: Chelsea, London

Intl debut: 27 June 2022 v South Africa (Test; Taunton)

A fast bowler, who can bowl at speeds in excess of 70 miles per hour (110 km/h), Issy comes from a cricketing family, with her mother Rachael a keen writer on the sport while two of her great-uncles played international cricket for Hong Kong. Growing up, Issy was part of a programme called Chance to Shine, which encouraged the participation in competitive cricket in state schools in the UK. In 2022, both Issy and Lauren Bell became the first Chance to Shine participants to play Test cricket for England. Issy has represented Birmingham Phoenix in The Hundred, Sydney Thunder in the Big Bash and signed for Indian Women's Premier League side Mumbai Indians in 2023.

CHARLIE DEAN

Role: Right-arm spin bowler; right-handed batter

DOB: 22 December 2000

POB: Burton-on-Trent, Staffordshire

Intl debut: 16 September 2021 v New Zealand (WODI; Bristol)

Charlie made an instant impression on her international debut with 10 wickets in the WODI series against New Zealand in autumn 2021. Her economical off-spin and reliable batting have made her one of the shining lights of the English domestic game, and she was instrumental in the Southern Vipers' maiden Charlotte Edwards Trophy victory in 2022. She also replaced the injured Heather Knight to captain London Spirit in The Hundred that same year. At international level, Charlie was England's leading wicket-taker in both their WODI and WT20I series against the West Indies in December 2022, with seven and 11 wickets respectively while she played in three matches in the 2023 Women's Ashes series, taking four wickets.

SOPHIE ECCLESTONE

Role: Slow left-arm spin bowler

DOB: 6 May 1999

POB: Chester, Cheshire

Intl debut: 3 July 2016 v Pakistan (WT20I; Bristol)

Having made her senior England debut in July 2016, Sophie took her 50th wicket in WT20Is and her 100th wicket in international cricket against the West Indies at the 2020 ICC Women's T20I World Cup. A bowler for the big occasion, Sophie shone during the 2022 ICC Women's World Cup. During the tournament, she took a total of 21 wickets - just two short of Lyn Fullston's all-time competition record. Her scalps included three back-to-back three-wicket hauls. Sophie's career-best 6-46 against South Africa in the semi-final match, took her to the top of England's World Cup wicket-taking rankings. Ecclestone was a standout performer in the multi-format 2023 Women's Ashes, taking a 10-wicket haul spanning across two innings on the fourth day of the five-day Test match.

SARAH GLENN

Role: Right-arm leg-spin bowler, right-handed batter

DOB: 27 August 1999

POB: Derby, Derbyshire

Intl debut: 9 December 2019 v Pakistan (WODI; Kuala Lumpur)

Soon after making her maiden international appearance in 2019, Sarah rose up the ICC T20I Bowling Rankings. She made the top 10 after an impressive display at the 2020 ICC Women's T20I World Cup which included taking 3-15 against Pakistan in England's penultimate group game. She reached second in those rankings in September 2022 behind teammate Sophie Ecclestone after taking a four-wicket haul against India. At the time of writing, Sarah is the ninth-highest wicket-taker of all time in WT20I with 59 in 49 matches.

England @ 2023 ICC Women's T20I World Cup

England Women headed to South Africa in February 2023 to compete in the eighth edition of the ICC Women's T20I World Cup.

BACKGROUND

England secured automatic qualification for the 2023 ICC Women's T20I World Cup by virtue of being one of the seven highest ranked teams in the ICC Women's T20I Rankings as of 30 November 2021. Australia, India, New Zealand, Sri Lanka, Pakistan and West Indies also qualified in this way, joining hosts South Africa and qualifying tournament winners Bangladesh and Ireland in the 10-team finals. England went into the competition with a decent pedigree, having won the first tournament in 2009 and been runners-up in 2012, 2014 and 2018.

England's 15 player squad for the tournament was:

Heather Knight (Captain)
Lauren Bell
Maia Bouchier
Alice Capsey
Kate Cross
Freya Davies
Charlie Dean
Sophia Dunkley
Sophie Ecclestone
Sarah Glenn
Amy Jones (Wicket Keeper)
Katherine Sciver-Brunt
Nat Sciver-Brunt (Vice-Captain)
Lauren Winfield-Hill (Wicket Keeper)
Danni Wyatt

Danielle Gibson and Issy Wong were named as travelling reserves.

GROUP STAGE

The tournament saw the 10 teams divided into two groups of five, with England joined by Ireland, India, Pakistan and West Indies in Group 2. The top two nations in each group progressed to the semi-finals of the competition while the other six teams were eliminated.

England got off to a good start in the tournament, beating the West Indies by seven wickets in their opening group fixture at Boland Park in Paarl on 11 February 2023. Sophie Ecclestone took three wickets for 23 runs while Player of the Match Nat Sciver-Brunt made 40* off 30 balls. The victory came less than 12 months on from England's seven-run defeat to the West Indies at the 2022 Women's Cricket World Cup.

A couple of days later, a dominant display against Ireland in Paarl made it two wins from two for England. Ecclestone took three wickets for 13 runs as Ireland were bowled out for 105 off 18.2 overs. Player of the Match Alice Capsey equalled the record for the fastest half-century in a Women's T20I World Cup match off 21 balls at the age of just 18. She was eventually caught by Leah Paul from Arlene Kelly for 51 off 22 balls as England hit 107 for 6 in 14.2 overs en route to a four-wicket victory.

An entertaining match saw England edge India to an 11-run win at St George's Park in Gqeberha on 18 February 2023. Batting first, England hit 151/7, with Nat Sciver-Brunt managing a half-century off 42 balls. In response, India managed 140/5 in their 20 overs.

England's score of 213/5 in their 114-run victory over Pakistan on 21 February 2023 was both the highest margin of victory (by runs) and total in a women's IT20 World Cup match. Nat Sciver-Brunt collected her third Player of the Match award at the tournament on a memorable afternoon at Newlands Cricket Ground in Cape Town.

Boasting a 100 per cent group record, England progressed to the tournament semi-finals along with group runners-up, India. Australia topped Group 1 while South Africa finished second.

The final Group 2 table was:

Pos	Team	Pld	W	L	T	NR	Pts	NRR
1	England	4	4	0	0	0	8	2.860
2	India	4	3	1	0	0	6	0.253
3	West Indies	4	2	2	0	0	4	−0.601
4	Pakistan	4	1	3	0	0	2	−0.703
5	Ireland	4	0	4	0	0	0	−1.814

SEMI-FINAL

England took on hosts South Africa in the semi-finals in Cape Town on 24 February 2023. South Africa won the toss and elected to bat first, hitting 164/4 in their 20 overs, despite Ecclestone taking three wickets for 22 runs. Tazmin Brits was in inspired form for South Africa, hitting 68 off 55 balls before she was eventually dismissed – caught by Katherine Sciver-Brunt off Lauren Bell. Brits' Player of the Match performance extended to her fielding display as she made four catches from Danni Wyatt, Sophia Dunkley, Capsey and Nat Sciver-Brunt, equalling the record for the highest number of catches in a WT20I match. South Africa progressed to the final with a 6-run victory over England, where they met Australia at Newlands Cricket Ground. Beth Mooney's 74* helped the Aussies to a 19-run win and their sixth competition triumph. Both Nat Sciver-Brunt and Ecclestone were subsequently named in the ICC's Team of the Tournament.

Semi-Final Scorecard | 24 February 2023

Newlands Cricket Ground, Cape Town

Umpires: **Claire Polosak** (Australia) and **Jacqueline Williams** (West Indies)

Player of the Match: **Tazmin Brits** (South Africa)

South Africa	England
164/4 (20 overs)	158/8 (20 overs)
Tazmin Brits 68 (55)	Nat Sciver-Brunt 40 (34)
Sophie Ecclestone 3/22 (4 overs)	Ayabonga Khaka 4/29 (4 overs)

SOUTH AFRICA WON BY 6 RUNS

2024 ICC Men's T20I World Cup Preview

The United States and West Indies will host the 20-team, Twenty20 International (T20I) tournament in the summer of 2024.

LOWDOWN

England will head to the United States and West Indies in the summer of 2024 to compete in the ninth ICC Men's T20I World Cup as reigning champions of the competition. With the 2024 tournament having been expanded from 16 to 20 teams, a total of 55 matches will take place during the Twenty20 International (T20I) tournament.

Five venues in the United States – likely to be Central Broward Regional Park Stadium in Florida, Moosa Stadium in Texas, the BPL Cricket Stadium in Illinois, Woodley Cricket Fields in California and the Indianapolis World Sports Park – are expected to stage around a third of the tournament's matches with the rest hosted at 13 different venues across the West Indies. Exact dates and venues for the competition were yet to be confirmed at the time of writing.

As of July 2023, 12 of the 20 competing nations for the competition had been confirmed with hosts United States and the West Indies joined by the top eight nations from the previous tournament - Australia, England, India, Netherlands, New Zealand, Pakistan, South Africa and Sri Lanka – and the two next highest-ranked teams, Afghanistan and Bangladesh. Qualification events were scheduled between late July and November 2023 to establish the other eight competing teams.

TOURNAMENT HISTORY

England have competed at all eight previous ICC T20I World Cup (previously known as ICC World Twenty20) tournaments, including the first in South Africa in 2007, which was won by India.

The Three Lions were victorious at the 2010 competition in the West Indies. They finished second to the West Indies but above Ireland in Group D to progress to the semi-final stage. A 7-wicket victory over Sri Lanka in St Lucia saw them into the final where they beat Australia by 7 wickets at the Kensington Oval in Bridgetown, Barbados. Kevin Pietersen was subsequently named Man of the Tournament having scored 248 runs across the four matches.

England staged the tournament in 2009, with Lord's, The Oval and Trent Bridge hosting the 27 matches. Pakistan beat Sri Lanka in the final while the Three Lions were unable to reach the knockout phase. Meanwhile Sri Lanka won the competition for the first time in Bangladesh in 2014 with a 6-wicket victory over India.

England and the West Indies are the most successful teams in ICC T20I World Cup history, having won the competition on two occasions each. The West Indies beat England in the final of the 2016 tournament in India, winning by 4 wickets and reaching their target with just two balls to spare. More on England's victory at the 2022 tournament in Australia can be found on pages 48 to 51 of this Annual.

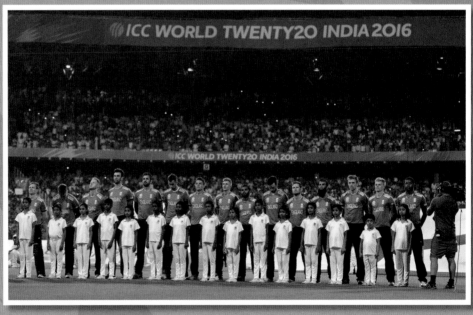

CROSSWORD

Can you name the non-sponsored versions of names of the various cricketing venues in England and Wales...?

Across

3 Southampton-based venue called the Ageas Bowl for sponsorship purposes (4-4)

7 The home of Surrey County Cricket Club (3-4)

8 This venue hosted the first senior game to be played under floodlights, as Warwickshire took on Somerset in 1997 (9)

9 Where England achieved their incredible 18-run victory over Australia in the 1981 Ashes (10)

11 Nottingham-based Test venue (5-6)

12 The churches of St James and St Mary Magdalene in Taunton can be seen from this venue (6-6)

Down

1 Known for sponsorship reasons as the Uptonsteel County Ground (5-4)

2 The venue known affectionately around the world as the 'Home of Cricket' (5)

4 Overlooked by Lumley Castle in Chester-le-Street (9-6)

5 This Greater Manchester cricket venue shares its name with a famous football ground (3-8)

6 The only England match venue based in Wales (6-7)

10 The home of Worcestershire County Cricket Club (3-4)

Find the solution on page 61

WORDSEARCH

Can you find the surnames of EIGHT England stars from the Men's and Women's teams? They can go horizontally, vertically or diagonally, forwards or backwards!

S	E	K	O	T	S	F	T	R	K	W	R	T
T	H	R	H	T	N	C	N	T	K	N	N	M
W	R	V	N	K	L	J	B	V	A	O	X	Y
T	F	B	P	P	J	Q	Q	Z	M	Y	X	P
V	Z	N	V	M	R	T	L	U	M	I	W	R
T	Z	V	G	L	T	Q	A	N	P	L	L	Q
W	D	C	L	M	L	E	Z	T	Q	A	L	T
F	K	U	E	K	B	K	B	V	T	T	M	F
Q	V	R	N	H	T	R	T	N	X	Y	N	K
L	W	Q	N	K	L	E	A	C	H	Y	P	M
K	T	Z	K	R	L	N	D	G	D	O	L	V
C	L	V	K	N	R	E	F	N	P	J	R	B
F	J	V	B	R	L	C	Y	E	M	H	Y	R

ALI   LEACH

BEAUMONT   POPE

DUNKLEY   STOKES

GLENN   WYATT

Find the solution on page 61

THE HOMES

In June 2023, the venues for several of England Men's and Women's international matches in the seven-year period from 2025 to 2031 were announced.

LORD'S

INDIA MEN'S TEST SERIES 2025 AND 2029

England Men's next Test series against India will take place at Lord's, The Kia Oval, Edgbaston, Headingley and Emirates Old Trafford while Lord's, The Kia Oval, Edgbaston, Emirates Old Trafford and The Ageas Bowl will host the Test series in 2029.

Known affectionately around the world as the 'Home of Cricket' – Lord's is where Middlesex County Cricket Club, the England and Wales Cricket Board (ECB) and the European Cricket Council (ECC) are based. Named after its founder, Thomas Lord, the present Lord's ground is about 250 yards north-west of the second Lord's venue, known as 'Lord's Middle Ground', which was used between 1811 and 1913. In addition to staging England Men's Test and ODI fixtures every year between 2025 and 2031, it will also stage a Women's white-ball fixture each year during that period.

KIA OVAL

Steeped in sporting history, The Kia Oval hosted England's first international football match on home soil against Scotland in 1870 and the first-ever FA Cup Final in 1872 as well as England rugby internationals against Wales and Scotland in 1876. The home of Surrey County Cricket Club, The Oval has staged almost 200 international matches to date, including over 100 Tests.

OF CRICKET

HEADINGLEY

Home to Yorkshire County Cricket Club, Headingley was the site of England's incredible 18-run victory over Australia in the 1981 Ashes, which featured Ian Botham's 149 not out. It was also where the Three Lions chased down their highest-ever fourth innings target to win 362-9 against Australia in the 2019 Ashes. The Leeds-based ground has over 120 years of international history, having staged its first Test between England and Australia on 29 June to 1 July 1899.

Emirates Old Trafford is England's second oldest Test venue after The Oval. It hosted the first Ashes Test in England in July 1884 and has staged more Cricket World Cup matches (17) than any other ground around the world. Many historic cricketing moments have occurred here, including the first 10-wicket haul in a single innings and a world record 19 wickets for 90 runs achieved by England bowler Jim Laker against Australia in 1956. The first of Sachin Tendulkar's 100 international centuries in 1990 and Shane Warne's so-called 'Ball of the Century' during the 1993 Ashes also took place at Old Trafford.

EMIRATES OLD TRAFFORD

EDGBASTON

The site of the first senior game to be played under floodlights, as Warwickshire took on Somerset in the Pro40 League in 1997, Edgbaston has hosted over 100 England matches to date, including 50-plus Tests. Its first Test took place on 29-31 May 1902, as the Three Lions faced Australia. More recently, it staged England's second Test against New Zealand in June 2021. In 2019, it was the setting for England's eight-wicket, semi-final victory over Australia during their triumphant 2019 ICC Cricket World Cup campaign.

Opened in 2001 on the outskirts of Southampton, The Ageas Bowl's first Test match was between England and Sri Lanka in 2011. More recently, in 2021, it hosted the final of the inaugural ICC World Test Championship which saw New Zealand beat India by eight wickets.

AGEAS BOWL

ASHES 2027 AND 2031

England Men will take on Australia in a five-Test series at Lord's, The Kia Oval, Edgbaston, Trent Bridge and The Ageas Bowl in 2027, with England Women meeting Australia Women in a Test match at Headingley as part of a multi-format series the same summer. In 2031, the Men's side will contest five Tests at Lord's, The Kia Oval, Emirates Old Trafford, Headingley and Trent Bridge, while the Women's multi-format series will include a Test match at The Ageas Bowl.

Trent Bridge gains its name from the nearby river crossing, which connects West Bridgford and Nottingham city centre. The ground hosted its first Test in 1899 as England took on Australia and it was where Stuart Broad took 8-15 in the same fixture in 2015. The venue for the final of the One-Day Cup up to and including 2024, Trent Bridge was also used to host the 2009 ICC T20I World Cup semi-final between South Africa and Pakistan.

TRENT BRIDGE

SEAT UNIQUE RIVERSIDE

ENGLAND WHITE-BALL FIXTURES 2025-2031

In addition to the grounds already mentioned, the Seat Unique Riverside, the Seat Unique Stadium and Sophia Gardens will host both England Men's and England Women's white-ball fixtures between 2025 and 2031.

Opened on a site overlooked by Lumley Castle in Chester-le-Street back in 1995, the Seat Unique Riverside hosted its first WODI between England and New Zealand in 1996, while its first men's Test saw England take on Zimbabwe in 2003.

Also known as the Bristol County Ground and Nevil Road, the Seat Unique Stadium is home to the Gloucestershire County Cricket Club and first staged England ODI and WODI matches in 1983 and 1984 respectively. A regular T20I and WT20I venue, the ground staged a Women's Test for the first time in 2021 as England took on India.

SEAT UNIQUE STADIUM

The only venue in Wales currently hosting England matches, Sophia Gardens in Cardiff first welcomed international cricket in May 1999 when Australia played New Zealand in the Cricket World Cup. It was named as one of three venues for the 2013 ICC Champions Trophy, staging five matches in total including the tournament opener between India and South Africa and was also a venue for the 2019 Cricket World Cup.

ALSO FEATURING...

Other grounds that will stage England Women's white-ball matches between 2025 and 2031 are:

Incora County Ground (Derby, Derbyshire)
The Cloud County Ground (Chelmsford, Essex)
The Spitfire Ground (Canterbury, Kent)
Uptonsteel County Ground (Leicester, Leicestershire)
The County Ground (Northampton, Northamptonshire)
Cooper Associates County Ground (Taunton, Somerset)
The 1st Central County Ground (Hove, East Sussex)
New Road (Worcester, Worcestershire)

SOPHIA GARDENS

All Stars Cricket

What is All Stars Cricket?

All Stars Cricket provides a fantastic first experience for all children aged 5-8 years old where they are guaranteed jam-packed fun, activity and skills development. The programme is designed to introduce children to the sport; teaching them new skills, helping them make new friends and have a great time along the way.

Every child that registers will receive a backpack full of goodies including:

- **Backpack**
- **Cricket bat**
- **Cricket ball**
- **Personalised t-shirt**

The Programme

There are over 2,200 clubs and centres registered to run All Stars courses - running both weekly courses and holiday camps - so you'll be guaranteed to find a session close to you when signing up.

Key course features include:

- **A perfect first experience of cricket for all children aged 5-8 years-old**
- **Eight weekly 60-minute sessions (or for Holiday Camps session durations vary)**
- **All Stars Cricket kit bag**
- **Valuable family time – parents/guardians are encouraged to take part too**

All Stars Cricket is fully inclusive and designed to support a wide range of abilities, disabilities and different learning needs.

Safe and fully accredited.

To find an All Stars Cricket club/centre close to you or for more information, visit: www.AllStarsCricket.co.uk

Dynamos Cricket

What is Dynamos Cricket?

Dynamos Cricket provides a fantastic next step for all those graduating from All Stars Cricket, but also the perfect introduction for all 8-11 year-olds new to the sport.

Complementing junior cricket, Dynamos helps develop skills such as bowling, batting and fielding, as well as providing lots of opportunity to play a game of Countdown Cricket. This means the children and their new friends can put their newly acquired skills to the test right away!

Every child who registers will receive their very own Dynamos Cricket New Balance t-shirt, personalised with their name and number.

Dynamos Cricket is fully inclusive and designed to support a wide range of abilities, disabilities and different learning needs.

Safe and fully accredited.

To find a Dynamos Cricket club/centre close to you or for more information, visit DynamosCricket.co.uk

The Programme

Key course features include:

- **Children will use soft balls and light wooden bats**
- **Minimum of six 60-90 minute sessions, or minimum eight hours of course delivery if it's a Dynamos Holiday Camp**
- **Introduction to game play through a countdown cricket match**
- **New Balance personalised t-shirt with name and number**
- **Valuable family time – parents/guardians are encouraged to take part too**
- **Complimentary digital app experience**
- **Exclusive access to Topps Cricket Attax cards**

ENGLAND QUIZ

Put your knowledge of England's men's and women's teams to the test with these 20 questions...

1. Which major tournament did England's Men win in 2022?

   1. _____

2. Which country staged the tournament mentioned in question one?

   2. _____

3. Who took an impressive 205 runs off just 208 deliveries in England Men's June 2023 Test victory against Ireland?

   3. _____

4. Who captained England at the 2023 ICC Women's T20I World Cup?

   4. _____

5. What is the name of the grassroots cricket programme designed for 8-11 year olds?

   5. _____

6. Who eliminated England Women from the 2023 ICC Women's T20I World Cup at the semi-final stage?

   6. _____

7. In what year did England win the ICC Women's T20I World Cup?

   7. _____

8. Who was appointed as England Women's Head Coach in 2022?

   8. _____

9. The West Indies and which other country will host the 2024 Men's T20I World Cup?

   9. _____

10. Prior to 2024, how many times had England previously won the Men's T20I World Cup?

    10. _____

11. What tournament did England Men win for the first time in 2019?

11.

12. Which Australian city hosted the inaugural Men's Test match between England and Australia in 1877?

12.

13. In what South African town did England play their first match at the 2023 ICC Women's T20I World Cup?

13.

14. The Ashes urn is reputed to contain the ashes of what? A – cricket bat, B – cricket bail or C – cricket ball

14.

15. Which ground hosted the first Test of the 2023 Men's Ashes between England and Australia in June 2023?

15.

16. Who became the second Englishman after Sir Alastair Cook to achieve 10,000 Test runs in June 2022?

16.

17. In which city was the only Test between England and Australia staged during the 2023 Women's Ashes series?

17.

18. Who scored 208 off 331 balls in the Women's Test between England and Australia in June 2023?

18.

19. In which city was Sophie Ecclestone born on 6 May 1999?

19.

20. What is the name of the grassroots cricket programme designed for 5-8 year olds?

20.

Find the answers on page 61

CHAMPIONS!

England were victorious at the 2022 ICC Men's T20I World Cup, which was staged in Australia between 16 October and 13 November 2022.

BACKGROUND

As one of 12 teams who reached the Super 12 phase of the 2021 ICC Men's T20I World Cup, England automatically qualified for the 2022 tournament along with Afghanistan, Australia, Bangladesh, India, Pakistan, New Zealand, South Africa, Namibia, Scotland, Sri Lanka and West Indies. The additional four teams that made up the 16-team tournament came from Global Qualifiers and they were Ireland, United Arab Emirates, Netherlands and Zimbabwe.

As outlined on pages 36 and 37, England had fared well at previous T20I World Cup finals, winning the competition in 2010 and finishing as runners-up in 2016.

England's 15 player squad was as follows;

Jos Buttler	Dawid Malan
(Captain, Wicket Keeper)	Tymal Mills
Moeen Ali	Adil Rashid
Harry Brook	Phil Salt
Sam Curran	Ben Stokes
Alex Hales	David Willey
Chris Jordan	Chris Woakes
Liam Livingstone	Mark Wood

From the squad originally announced, Jonny Bairstow and Reece Topley were replaced by Alex Hales and Tymal Mills respectively due to injury while Luke Wood travelled to the tournament as a reserve.

SUPER 12

England entered the tournament at the Super 12 stage and were placed in Group 1 along with Australia, New Zealand, Sri Lanka, Ireland and Afghanistan. Each team in the group met once with the top two nations advancing to the semi-final.

Jos Buttler's side enjoyed a winning start to the competition with a five-wicket victory over Afghanistan in Perth on 22 October 2022. Sam Curran was Player of the Match, as he took five wickets for 10 runs. In doing so, he became the first bowler for England to take a five-wicket haul in a T20I match. After bowling out Afghanistan for 112, England managed 113/5 in 18.1 overs.

With rain preventing any further play, Ireland secured a shock five-run victory (DLS method) in Melbourne on 26 October 2022. England were 105/5 after 14.3 overs when rain stopped play having bowled Ireland out for 157. Rain then prevented three Group 1 fixtures taking place at all, including Australia versus England on 28 October 2022.

A 20-run win over New Zealand at The Gabba on 1 November 2022 helped put England back on course for qualification for the semi-finals. Buttler was named Player of the Match as he hit 73 from 43 balls helping England to a total of 179/6. A place in the last four was sealed with a four-wicket victory over Sri Lanka four days later. Australia were eliminated from the tournament in the process as England snatched the runners-up spot in Group 1 by virtue of a better net run rate while New Zealand topped the group. In Group 2, India finished top while Pakistan were second.

The final Group 1 table was:

Pos	Team	Pld	W	L	NR	Pts	NRR
1	New Zealand	5	3	1	1	7	2.113
2	England	5	3	1	1	7	0.473
3	Australia	5	3	1	1	7	−0.173
4	Sri Lanka	5	2	3	0	4	−0.422
5	Ireland	5	1	3	1	3	−1.615
6	Afghanistan	5	0	3	2	2	−0.571

SEMI-FINAL

A 170-run partnership between Buttler and Alex Hales – a record for a men's T20I World Cup match – saw England to an incredible 10-wicket victory over India in the semi-final in Adelaide on 10 November 2022. Set a target of 169 to secure a place in the final, Alex Hales hit 86* – including four 4s and seven 6s - off 47 balls, while Buttler's 80* included nine 4s and three 6s.

Semi-Final Scorecard | 10 NOVEMBER 2022

Adelaide Oval, Adelaide

Umpires: **Kumar Dharmasena** (Sri Lanka) and **Paul Reiffel** (Australia)

Player of the Match: **Alex Hales** (England)

India	England
168/6 (20 overs)	170/0 (16 overs)
Hardik Pandya 63 (33)	**Alex Hales** 86* (47)
Chris Jordan 3/43 (4 overs)	

ENGLAND WON BY 10 WICKETS

CHAMPIONS

A crowd of 80,462 at Melbourne Cricket Ground watched a pulsating ICC Men's T20I World Cup Final between England and Pakistan. England won the toss and elected to field with Pakistan scoring 137 runs for the fall of eight wickets with Player of the Match Sam Curran taking three wickets for 12 runs. With the scores level after Ben Stokes brought up

his maiden T20I fifty, he then scored the winning runs with six balls to spare. Buttler's team's triumph saw England become the first men's team to hold both the ODI and T20I World Cup titles simultaneously.

Curran went on to be named Player of the Tournament with Buttler, Hales and Mark Wood all named in the Team of the Tournament.

Final Scorecard | 13 NOVEMBER 2022

Melbourne Cricket Ground, Melbourne

Umpires: **Kumar Dharmasena** (Sri Lanka) and **Marais Erasmus** (South Africa)

Player of the Match: **Sam Curran** (England)

Pakistan	England
137/8 (20 overs)	138/5 (19 overs)
Shan Masood 38 (28)	**Ben Stokes** 52* (49)
Sam Curran 3/12 (4 overs)	**Haris Rauf** 2/23 (4 overs)

ENGLAND WON BY 5 WICKETS

England toured New Zealand in February 2023 and faced the Black Caps in a tour match against a New Zealand XI and two full Tests. Harry Brook was England's player of the series, scoring 89 off 81 balls in the first Test victory at the Bay Oval in Mount Maunganui; he followed that up with a mammoth 186 in the second Test in Wellington. A number of landmarks were achieved during the first Test, with James Anderson and Stuart Broad becoming the highest wicket takers as a pair in Tests, surpassing the Warne-McGrath record of 1001 wickets. Meanwhile Ben Stokes surpassed Kiwi Brendon McCullum's record of 107 sixes to become the highest six hitter in Test cricket.

SCORECARD

Tour Match (v New Zealand XI) | 8-9 February 2023

Seddon Park, Hamilton

Umpires: **Chris Brown** (New Zealand) and **Tim Parlane** (New Zealand)

England	New Zealand XI
465 (69.2 overs)	310 (82.1 overs)
Harry Brook 97 (71)	**Quinn Sunde** 91 (128)
Kyle Jamieson 3/65 (15 overs)	**Olly Stone** 3/54 (11.1 overs)

MATCH DRAWN

1st Test | 16-20 February 2023

Bay Oval, Mount Maunganui

Umpires: **Aleem Dar** (Pakistan) and **Chris Gaffaney** (New Zealand)

Player of the Match: **Harry Brook** (England)

England	New Zealand
325/9d (58.2 overs)	306 (82.5 overs)
Harry Brook 89 (81)	**Tom Blundell** 138 (181)
Neil Wagner 4/82 (16.2 overs)	**Ollie Robinson** 4/54 (19 overs)
374 (73.5 overs)	126 (45.3 overs)
Joe Root 57 (62)	**Daryl Mitchell** 57* (101)
Blair Tickner 3/55 (12 overs)	**James Anderson** 4/18 (10.3 overs)

ENGLAND WON BY 267 RUNS

2nd Test | 24-28 February 2023

Basin Reserve, Wellington

Umpires: **Chris Gaffaney** (New Zealand) and **Rod Tucker** (Australia)

Player of the Match: **Kane Williamson** (NZ)

England	New Zealand
435/8d (87.1 overs)	209 (53.2 overs)
Harry Brook 186 (176)	**Tim Southee** 73 (49)
Matt Henry 4/100 (22.1 overs)	**Stuart Broad** 4/61 (14.2 overs)
256 (74.2 overs)	483 (162.3 overs) (f/o)
Joe Root 95 (113)	**Kane Williamson** 132 (282)
Neil Wagner 4/62 (15.2 overs)	**Jack Leach** 5/157 (61.3 overs)

NEW ZEALAND WON BY 1 RUN

TEST SERIES DRAWN 1-1

MATCH ACTION

Ashes Series 2023
16 June – 31 July 2023

The 73rd Men's Ashes and 25th Women's Ashes took place in the summer of 2023 as old rivals England and Australia locked horns once again.

MEN'S ASHES

Edgbaston, Lord's, Headingley, Emirates Old Trafford and The Kia Oval hosted the five Tests of the 2023 LV= Insurance Men's Ashes Series. Despite Joe Root's 118* in the first innings of the opening match at Edgbaston, Australia secured a two-wicket victory. Man of the Match Usman Khawaja became just the second Australian player and 13th player overall to bat on all five days of a Test match as he reached 141 off 321 balls in the first innings and 65 for 197 in the second.

Ben Stokes produced an impressive performance in the second Test with his second innings containing nine sixes - the most in an Ashes innings. But Australia claimed victory at Lord's by 43 runs. England responded with victory in the third Test at

Headingley, bowler Mark Wood receiving Man of the Match after taking 5-34 in the first innings. The host nation were in a strong position in the fourth Test too, with 592 runs off 107.4 overs before rain stopped play. Australia retained the Ashes as the match at Old Trafford finished in a draw.

Stuart Broad took his 600th Test wicket in the fourth Test, becoming just the fifth bowler to reach the milestone in the process. Prior to the fifth Test at The Oval, he announced his retirement from all forms of cricket. In his farewell match - the final day of the fifth Test on 31 July 2023 - Broad hit a six from the last ball he faced, then took a wicket with the final ball he bowled as England won the Test and drew the series 2-2.

SCORECARD

1st Test | 16-20 June 2023

Edgbaston, Birmingham

Umpires: **Marais Erasmus** (South Africa) and **Ahsan Raza** (Pakistan)

England	Australia
393/8d (78 overs)	386 (116.1 overs)
Joe Root 118* (152)	**Usman Khawaja** 141 (321)
Nathan Lyon 4/149 (29 overs)	**Ollie Robinson** 3/55 (22.1 overs)
273 (66.2 overs)	282/8 (92.3 overs)
Harry Brook 46 (52)	**Usman Khawaja** 65 (197)
Pat Cummins 4/63 (18.2 overs)	**Stuart Broad** 3/64 (21 overs)
AUSTRALIA WON BY TWO WICKETS	

2nd Test | 28 June-2 July 2023

Lord's, London

Umpires: **Chris Gaffaney** (New Zealand) and **Ahsan Raza** (Pakistan)

Player of the Match: **Steve Smith** (Australia)

Australia	England
416 (100.4 overs)	325 (76.2 overs)
Steve Smith 110 (184)	**Ben Duckett** 98 (134)
Josh Tongue 3/98 (22 overs)	**Mitchell Starc** 3/88 (17 overs)
279 (101.5 overs)	327 (81.3 overs)
Usman Khawaja 77 (187)	**Ben Stokes** 155 (214)
Stuart Broad 4/65 (24.5 overs)	**Pat Cummins** 3/69 (25 overs)
AUSTRALIA WON BY 43 RUNS	

3rd Test | 6-10 July 2023

Headingley, Leeds
Umpires: **Kumar Dharmasena** (Sri Lanka) and **Nitin Menon** (India)
Player of the Match: **Mark Wood** (England)

Australia	England
263 (60.4 overs)	237 (52.3 overs)
Mitchell Marsh 118 (118)	**Ben Stokes** 80 (108)
Mark Wood 5/34 (11.4 overs)	**Pat Cummins** 6/91 (18 overs)
224 (67.1 overs)	254/7 (50 overs)
Travis Head 77 (112)	**Harry Brook** 75 (93)
Stuart Broad 3/45 (14.1 overs)	**Mitchell Starc** 5/78 (16 overs)

ENGLAND WON BY 3 WICKETS

4th Test | 19-23 July 2023

Emirates Old Trafford, Manchester

Umpires: **Nitin Menon** (India) and **Joel Wilson** (West Indies)

Player of the Match: **Zak Crawley** (England)

Australia	England
317 (90.2 overs)	592 (107.4 overs)
Mitchell Marsh 51 (60)	**Zak Crawley** 189 (182)
Chris Woakes 5/62 (22.2 overs)	**Josh Hazlewood** 5/126 (27 overs)
214/5 (71 overs)	
Marnus Labuschagne 111 (173)	
Mark Wood 3/27 (11 overs)	

MATCH DRAWN

5th Test | 27-31 July 2023

The Kia Oval, London

Umpires: **Kumar Dharmasena** (Sri Lanka) and **Joel Wilson** (West Indies)

Player of the Match: **Chris Woakes** (England)

England	Australia
283 (54.4 overs)	295 (103.1 overs)
Harry Brook 85 (91)	**Steve Smith** 71 (123)
Mitchell Starc 4/82 (14.4 overs)	**Chris Woakes** 3/61 (25 overs)
395 (81.5 overs)	334 (94.4 overs)
Joe Root 91 (106)	**Usman Khawaja** 72 (145)
Mitchell Starc 4/100 (20 overs)	**Chris Woakes** 4/50 (19 overs)

ENGLAND WON BY 49 RUNS

TEST SERIES DRAWN 2-2

WOMEN'S ASHES

The centrepiece of the 2023 Metro Bank Women's Ashes Series was a single Test which took place at Trent Bridge on 22-26 June 2023. Lauren Filer and Danni Wyatt both made their Test debuts in the match while Tammy Beaumont became the first English batter to score a double century in a women's Test during the match. Despite Sophie Ecclestone taking her first five and ten-wicket Test hauls in the match, Australia - inspired by Player of the Match Ashleigh Gardner, who matched Ecclestone's feat - won by 89 runs.

Both the One Day International Series and Twenty20 International Series resulted in 2-1 victories for England though, as the overall Women's Ashes Series ended in a draw, both teams earning eight points. Nat Sciver-Brunt scored 271 runs across the WODI Series while Wyatt hit 109 in the WT20I Series to claim the respective Player of the Series awards. Ecclestone took her 100th wicket in WT20Is in the second match of the Series while England's victory in the first WODI in Bristol on 12 July 2023 was notable for England's highest successful run chase in a WODI, as they responded to Australia's 263-8 with a score of 267-8.

SCORECARD

Only Test | 22-26 June 2023

Trent Bridge, Nottingham

Umpires: **Anna Harris** (England) and **Sue Redfern** (England)

Player of the Match: **Ashleigh Gardner** (Australia)

Australia	England
473 (124.2 overs)	463 (121.2 overs)
Annabel Sutherland 137* (184)	**Tammy Beaumont** 208 (331)
Sophie Ecclestone 5/129 (46.2 overs)	**Ashleigh Gardner** 4/99 (25.2 overs)
257 (78.5 overs)	178 (49 overs)
Beth Mooney 85 (168)	**Danni Wyatt** 54 (88)
Sophie Ecclestone 5/63 (30.5 overs)	**Ashleigh Gardner** 8/66 (20 overs)

AUSTRALIA WON BY 89 RUNS

WT20I

SCORECARD

1st WT20I | 1 July 2023

Edgbaston, Birmingham

Umpires: **Anna Harris** (England) and **Sue Redfern** (England)

Player of the Match: **Beth Mooney** (Australia)

England	Australia
153/7 (20 overs)	154/6 (19.5 overs)
Sophia Dunkley 56 (49)	**Beth Mooney** 61* (47)
Jess Jonassen 3/25 (4 overs)	**Sophie Ecclestone** 2/24 (3.5 overs)

AUSTRALIA WON BY FOUR WICKETS

2nd WT20I | 5 July 2023

The Kia Oval, London

Umpires: **Jasmine Naeem** (England) and **Russell Warren** (England)

Player of the Match: **Danni Wyatt** (England)

England	Australia
186/9 (20 overs)	183/8 (20 overs)
Danni Wyatt 76 (46)	**Ellyse Perry** 51* (27)
Annabel Sutherland 3/28 (4 overs)	**Sarah Glenn** 2/27 (4 overs)

ENGLAND WON BY THREE RUNS

3rd WT20I | 8 July 2023

Lord's, London

Umpires: **Sue Redfern** (England) and **Russell Warren** (England)

Player of the Match: **Alice Capsey** (England)

Australia	England
155/7 (20 overs)	121/5 (13.2 overs)
Ellyse Perry 34 (25)	**Alice Capsey** 46 (23)
Nat Sciver-Brunt 2/31 (4 overs)	**Megan Schutt** 2/35 (3 overs)

ENGLAND WON BY FIVE WICKETS (DLS METHOD)

1st WODI | 12 July 2023

County Ground, Bristol

Umpires: **Anna Harris** (England) and **Sue Redfern** (England)

Player of the Match: **Heather Knight** (England)

Australia	England
263/8 (50 overs)	267/8 (48.1 overs)
Beth Mooney 81* (99)	**Heather Knight** 75* (86)
Nat Sciver-Brunt 2/38 (8 overs)	**Ashleigh Gardner** 3/42 (10 overs)

ENGLAND WON BY TWO WICKETS

2nd WODI | 16 July 2023

The Ageas Bowl, Southampton

Umpires: **Mike Burns** (England) and **Jasmine Naeem** (England)

Player of the Match: **Alana King** (Australia)

Australia	England
282/7 (50 overs)	279/7 (50 overs)
Ellyse Perry 91 (124)	**Nat Sciver-Brunt** 111* (99)
Sophie Ecclestone 3/40 (10 overs)	**Alana King** 3/44 (10 overs)

AUSTRALIA WON BY THREE RUNS

3rd WODI | 18 July 2023

County Ground, Taunton

Umpires: **Mike Burns** (England) and **Anna Harris** (England)

Player of the Match: **Nat Sciver-Brunt** (England)

England	Australia
285/9 (50 overs)	199 (35.3 overs)
Nat Sciver-Brunt 129 (149)	**Ellyse Perry** 53 (58)
Jess Jonassen 3/30 (5 overs)	**Kate Cross** 3/48 (8 overs)

ENGLAND WON BY 69 RUNS (DLS METHOD)

ASHES SERIES TIED WITH EIGHT POINTS EACH

MATCH ACTION

Ireland in England
1 June - 26 September 2023

Ireland visited England for a single Test match which took place at Lord's on 1-4 June 2023. In preparation for the game, the tourists faced Essex in a three-day first-class match at the County Ground, Chelmsford between 26-28 May 2023 and won by 10 wickets. Ahead of the Test, James Anderson and Ollie Robinson were both ruled out through injury with Josh Tongue added to the England squad as a result.

The Test match saw England win the toss and they elected to field first. This strategy paid off as Stuart Broad secured an early wicket – trapping PJ Moor LBW – and completed a five-wicket haul on Day 1.

England put on a dominant batting performance, declaring their innings on Day 2 at 524 after the dismissal of Ollie Pope. Pope took an impressive 205 runs off just 208 deliveries while Ben Duckett scored 182 off 178 balls. Pope achieved several milestones during his innings which included England's fastest double-century on home soil.

Ireland's second innings saw Tongue claim his maiden Test wicket when PJ Moor was trapped LBW once again. He took two further wickets on both Day 2 and 3, completing a five-wicket haul on his Test debut. Victory was sealed as Zak Crawley hit three boundaries in four deliveries for a 10-wicket triumph. Pope was named Player of the Match on the back of his double-century.

Ireland returned to England for three ODI matches between 20-26 September 2023, after this Annual went to print.

ODI SERIES V IRELAND

1ST ODI - 20 September 2023
– Headingley, Leeds

2ND ODI – 23 September 2023
– Trent Bridge, Nottingham

3RD ODI – 26 September 2023
– County Ground, Bristol

SCORECARD

Only Test | 1-4 June 2023

Lord's, London

Umpires: **Adrian Holdstock** (South Africa) and **Paul Wilson** (Australia)

Player of the Match: **Ollie Pope** (England)

Ireland	England
172 (56.2 overs)	524/4d (82.4 overs)
James McCollum 36 (108)	**Ollie Pope** 205 (208)
Stuart Broad 5/51 (17 overs)	**Andy McBrine** 2/99 (13.4 overs)
362 (86.2 overs)	12/0 (0.4 overs)
Mark Adair 88 (76)	**Zak Crawley** 12* (4)
Josh Tongue 5/66 (21 overs)	

ENGLAND WON BY 10 WICKETS

QUIZ AND PUZZLE ANSWERS

PAGE 10 – SPOT THE DIFFERENCE

PAGE 11 – SPOT THE BALL

PAGE 11 – WORD GRID

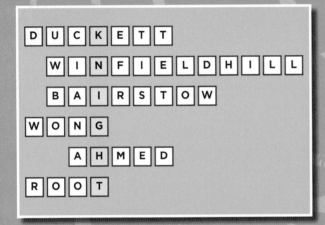

PAGE 38 – CROSSWORD

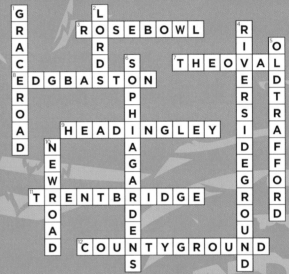

PAGE 39 – WORDSEARCH

PAGE 46-47 – ENGLAND QUIZ

1) T20I World Cup
2) Australia
3) Ollie Pope
4) Heather Knight
5) Dynamos Cricket
6) South Africa
7) 2009
8) Jon Lewis
9) United States
10) Twice
11) Cricket World Cup
12) Melbourne
13) Paarl
14) B – cricket bail
15) Edgbaston
16) Joe Root
17) Nottingham
18) Tammy Beaumont
19) Chester
20) All Stars Cricket

WE ARE
**ENGLAND
CRICKET**